Revitalizing Renal Recipes

A Cookbook for Kidney Health

Alicia Asprey

Copyright © 2023 - All rights reserved.

The content contained within this book may not be reproduced, duplicated, or transmitted without direct written permission from the author or the publisher.

Under no circumstances will any blame or legal responsibility be held against the publisher, or author, for any damages, reparation, or monetary loss due to the information contained within this book. Either directly or indirectly.

Legal Notice:

This book is copyright protected. This book is only for personal use. You cannot amend, distribute, sell, use, quote, or paraphrase any part, or the content within this book, without the consent of the author or publisher.

Disclaimer Notice:

Please note the information contained within this document is for educational and entertainment purposes only. All effort has been executed to present accurate, up-to-date, and reliable, complete information. No warranties of any kind are declared or implied. Readers acknowledge that the author is not engaging in the rendering of legal, financial, medical, or professional advice. The content within this book has been derived from various sources. Please consult a licensed professional before attempting any techniques outlined in this book.

By reading this document, the reader agrees that under no circumstances is the author responsible for any losses, direct or indirect, which are incurred as a result of the use of the information contained within this document, including, but not limited to, — errors, omissions, or inaccuracies.

Table of Content

Grasping the Fundamentals of Kidney Disease

What Does Kidney Disease Entail? Kidney disease falls into two broad categories. The first, acute kidney injury, refers to sudden damage to the kidneys. The second, chronic kidney disease, represents the slow decline of kidney function over time. A person suffering from acute kidney injury is more prone to developing chronic kidney disease and vice versa. The glomerular filtration rate (GFR) serves as the most effective way to measure kidney functionality.

GFR is a tool to measure kidney function and determine the severity of kidney failure. This equation uses patient data such as race, age, gender, and serum creatinine level. Creatinine is a waste product produced by muscle usage. As kidney function decreases, the creatinine level in the blood increases because the kidneys can no longer efficiently filter and excrete waste.

Emphasizing Kidney Health For optimal functioning, the kidney must provide the body with the correct amount of water. One of the key tasks of the kidneys is to expel excess water from the body or retain it when more is needed.

Balance of chemicals in the blood and body fluids is critical for proper body function. Sodium (salt) and potassium, for instance, are minerals derived from food. The body needs these minerals for its health, but they must be conserved in specific quantities. When the kidneys are functioning correctly, surplus food elements, including sodium and potassium, exit the body through urine. The kidneys also help adjust the amounts of other minerals, such as calcium and phosphate, which are vital for bone formation, strength, and other functions.

The kidneys aid in the removal of waste substances such as creatinine and urea from the body. These wastes are produced when the body breaks down proteins like meat. Creatinine is a waste product of muscle. As kidney activity decreases, urea and creatinine levels in the blood increase. The blood creatinine level is a valuable measure of kidney function and can be determined through direct blood analysis.

Healthy kidneys also produce vital hormones in the body. These hormones travel through the bloodstream as "messengers," regulating the body's blood pressure, red blood cell production, and calcium balance.

When living with chronic kidney disease (CKD), you may need to adjust your diet. These changes may include limiting fluids, eating a low-protein diet, restricting sodium, potassium, phosphorus, or other electrolytes, and consuming enough calories if you are losing weight.

As your kidney disease progresses or if you require dialysis, you may need to further modify your diet. This is where the renal diet comes into play. The renal diet aims to maintain a balance of electrolytes, nutrients, and fluids in your body when you are undergoing dialysis for chronic kidney disease.

Those on dialysis need this specialized diet to limit the accumulation of waste products in the body. Fluid restriction between dialysis sessions is crucial, as most individuals on dialysis have little or no urine output. Without urination, pressure builds up in the body, leading to excessive blood in the heart and lungs.

Harnessing the Power of Diet for Kidney Health Why Diet Matters for Kidney Health When the kidneys aren't functioning properly, fluid and waste build up in your body. Over time, this excess fluid and waste can harm your heart, bones, and other organs. A kidney-friendly diet limits the intake of certain nutrients and fluids to prevent fluid and waste from accumulating and causing problems.

Depending on the stage of your kidney disease, your diet needs to be as strict as possible. In the early stages of kidney disease, you may have few, if any, restrictions on what you can eat or drink. However, as your kidney disease worsens, your doctor may advise you to limit your intake of phosphorus, fluids, and potassium.

Determining Nutrients to Limit or Avoid The degree of dietary restriction depends on the extent of kidney damage. For instance, people with early-stage kidney disease have different limitations than those with severe kidney impairment, known as End-stage renal disease (ESRD). If you have kidney disease, your healthcare provider can advise on the most suitable diet for you. Most individuals with chronic kidney disease need to follow a kidney-friendly diet, also known as a renal diet, which helps control the amounts of waste in their blood, improve kidney function, and prevent further damage. Though dietary restrictions vary, all individuals with kidney disease are advised to monitor the following nutrients:

Sodium

One of the crucial nutrients you need to monitor closely is sodium. When the kidneys aren't working properly, they can't maintain the body's balance of water and sodium. That's why the renal diet calls for limiting salt and fluid intake. Consuming too much sodium can increase thirst, which in turn makes it harder to limit fluid intake. The American Heart Association suggests that adults should not consume more than 2300 mg of sodium per day, which reduces further to 1500 mg for anyone with hypertension or kidney disorders. To put this in perspective, 2300 mg of sodium is present in just one teaspoon of salt, including kosher and sea salt.

Increased sodium intake is linked to high blood pressure or hypertension, which can lead to stiffening and narrowing of blood vessels, impairing the supply of oxygen to organs. This results in the heart working harder to pump blood, increasing blood pressure. If left uncontrolled, this condition can compromise cardiovascular function. High blood pressure also puts more strain on the kidneys, damaging the filtering unit and worsening their ability to regulate fluid balance. This exacerbates any existing kidney disorders and poses risks to cardiovascular health.

Phosphorus

Phosphorus is a vital mineral that aids in maintaining the strength and health of bones and muscles. The small intestines absorb the phosphorus needed by the bones, and the kidneys remove any excess. When the kidneys fail to remove the extra phosphorus, it starts to accumulate in the blood. This leads to calcium being leached from the bones, weakening them. Excessive phosphorus levels can also cause calcium deposits in the lungs, heart, kidneys, and blood vessels. High phosphorus intake can worsen kidney disease and increase the risk of cardiovascular diseases and mortality. So, keeping your phosphorus levels low is essential when following the renal diet.

Potassium

Potassium is a vital electrolyte required for the body's overall functioning. This mineral is commonly found in most foods and is necessary for different functions, including regular heartbeat and muscle functioning. The kidneys regulate potassium levels in the body, removing any surplus in the urine. When the kidneys fail to function properly, they can't control potassium levels, leading to a condition called hyperkalemia, characterized by excessive potassium. There's a direct relationship between increased potassium intake and the risk of chronic kidney disease.

Hyperkalemia can cause irregular heartbeat, slowed pulse, muscle weakness, and increase the risk of heart attacks, strokes, and in severe cases, even death. Therefore, learning to limit potassium intake is crucial for improving kidney health. This involves limiting consumption of potassium-rich foods and avoiding certain foods altogether due to their high potassium content.

Protein

Protein is a vital macronutrient required for overall body function and health. It aids in tissue repair, muscle building, and fighting infections. If your kidneys aren't functioning properly, you need to be mindful of your protein intake, both in terms of quantity and quality. Consuming too much protein or poor-quality protein can increase waste in the blood, adding stress to the kidneys and potentially damaging them. The amount of protein you need to consume varies depending on your stage of kidney disease. As a general rule, you should opt for high-quality, lean protein.

Vitamin and Mineral Supplements

If you have kidney disease, over-the-counter multivitamins might not be suitable for your health. You may need to limit or avoid vitamins A, E, and K as levels of these vitamins build up in the body as kidney function decreases. It's advisable to consult your doctor about the necessity and safety of vitamin and mineral supplements.

Fluids

Depending on the health of your kidneys and your recovery rate, your doctor might recommend reducing your fluid intake. This could necessitate a reduction in foods that are high in water content. Soups and foods that melt, like ice, ice cream, and gelatin, contain a lot of water. Many fruits and vegetables are also high in water content.

Typically, people with severe renal failure are advised to limit their fluid intake to about four cups daily, or as prescribed by your physician. It's important to note that everyone with kidney issues has unique dietary needs, so it's crucial to discuss your specific requirements with your doctor. Thankfully, there are plenty of tasty and nutritious options that are low in phosphate, potassium, and sodium.

The Power of Diet in Kidney Health

The Role of Diet in Kidney Health When the kidneys aren't functioning properly, fluid and waste build up in the body. Over time, this excess fluid and waste can damage your heart, bones, and other organs. A kidney-friendly diet restricts the consumption of certain nutrients and fluids to prevent the accumulation of fluid and waste, thus averting potential problems.

Depending on the stage of your kidney disease, your dietary regimen should be as strict as possible. In the early stages of kidney disease, you may have minimal or no restrictions on what you eat and drink. However, as your kidney disease progresses, your doctor may advise you to limit your intake of phosphorus, fluids, and potassium.

Your dietary restrictions may change further if your kidney disease worsens, or if you need to start dialysis. This is when the renal diet becomes particularly crucial. The aim of the renal diet is to balance the amounts of electrolytes, nutrients, and fluids in your body when you are undergoing dialysis for chronic kidney disease.

People on dialysis need this special diet to limit the buildup of waste products in their bodies. Restricting fluid intake between dialysis treatments is crucial, as most people on dialysis produce little to no urine. Without urination, pressure in the body can increase, leading to an excess of blood in the heart and lungs.

Why Diet is Critical for Kidney Health

When kidneys are not functioning properly, fluid and waste build up in your body. Over time, the extra fluid and waste can damage your heart, bones, and other organs. A kidney-friendly diet limits the intake of certain nutrients and fluids to prevent fluid and waste from building up and causing problems.

Depending on the stage of your kidney disease, your diet should be as strict as possible. You might have few or no restrictions on what you can eat and drink in the early stages of kidney disease. But as your kidney disease gets worse, your doctor might recommend that you limit phosphorus, fluids, and potassium.

If your kidney disease gets worse or if you need dialysis, you might need to change your diet even more. That's where the renal diet comes into play. The purpose of the renal diet is to maintain the levels of electrolytes, nutrients, and fluids in your body when you're on dialysis for chronic kidney disease.

People on dialysis need this special diet to limit the buildup of waste products in their bodies. Limiting fluid between dialysis treatments is very important because most people on dialysis have little or no urine output.

Without urination, pressure within the body can build up, leading to an excess volume of blood in the heart and lungs.

Nutrients to Limit or Avoid

The extent of kidney damage determines the dietary limitations. For instance, people with early-stage kidney disease have different dietary restrictions compared to those with severe kidney damage, also known as Endstage renal disease (ESRD). If you have kidney disease, your healthcare provider can determine the appropriate diet for you. Most patients with chronic kidney disease need to follow a kidney-friendly diet that limits the excess amounts of certain substances in their blood. This diet, also known as a renal diet, aids in improving kidney function and preventing further damage.

Though dietary restrictions vary, all individuals with kidney disease are advised to limit the following nutrients:

Sodium

One of the most important nutrients to monitor closely is sodium. When kidneys are not functioning as they should, their ability to maintain a balance of water and sodium in the body is compromised. This is why it is essential to limit your intake of salt and fluids on a renal diet. Consuming excess sodium increases thirst, which in turn makes it challenging to limit fluids. The American Heart Association recommends that adults should not consume more than 2300 mg of sodium per day, and this limit decreases to 1500 mg for those with hypertension or kidney disorders. To put things into perspective, a teaspoon of salt, including kosher and sea salt, contains 2300 mg of sodium.

Phosphorus

Phosphorus is an essential mineral that aids in maintaining the strength and health of bones and muscles. The small intestine absorbs the phosphorus needed by the bones, and the kidneys remove any excess phosphorus. When the kidneys are unable to eliminate the extra phosphorus, it begins to accumulate in the blood. This excessive build-up of phosphorus in the blood can lead to the leaching of calcium from the bones, weakening them. Increased intake of phosphorus not only worsens the progression of kidney diseases but also increases the risk of cardiovascular diseases and mortality. Therefore, maintaining low phosphorus levels is crucial while following the renal diet.

Potassium

Potassium is one of the three essential electrolytes required for the overall functioning of the human body. This mineral, found in most foods, is needed for various functions including ensuring regular heartbeat and muscle function. The kidneys regulate the levels of potassium in the body. Healthy kidneys know exactly how much potassium is needed and remove any excess in the urine. When the kidneys aren't functioning as they should, they can't control the level of potassium, leading to hyperkalemia, a condition characterized by higher than normal potassium levels. There's a direct correlation between high potassium intake and the risk of chronic kidney disease.

Protein

Protein is one of the three essential macronutrients necessary for overall health and functioning of the body. It aids in tissue repair, muscle building, and fighting infections. If your kidneys aren't functioning properly, you need to be mindful of your protein intake. This isn't just about the quantity but also the quality of protein you consume. Excess protein consumption or consuming poor-quality protein can harm kidney health and function.

Fluids

Depending on the health of your kidneys and the rate at which they recover, your doctor might advise you to reduce your fluid intake. This could mean reducing foods that have high water content, such as soups, and foods that melt, like ice, ice cream, and gelatin. Many fruits and vegetables also have a high water content.

Individuals with kidney issues have unique dietary needs, so it's important to discuss your specific requirements with your doctor. Luckily, there are many delicious and nutritious options that are low in phosphate, potassium, and sodium.

NUTRIENTS TO FOCUS ON AND CONSUME IN CONTROLLED AMOUNTS

A diet suitable for kidney health calls for specific attention to certain nutrients to prevent further strain on the kidneys and additional damage to the body. While there are some nutrients you need to monitor or limit, there are also foods that you should aim to include more in your diet.

Beneficial Carbohydrates and Whole Grains

Carbohydrates are essential for providing your body with the energy it requires to perform effectively. In particular, glucose, a type of carbohydrate, is the brain's preferred energy source. There are different categories of carbohydrates—starches, sugars, and fiber—all of which can be part of a balanced diet.

Whole grains should be a significant component of the carbohydrates in your diet. In the past, due to their high phosphorus content, whole grains were not advised for individuals with kidney disease. However, more recent research suggests that the phosphorus in whole grains isn't as readily broken down and absorbed in the human body. Whole grains are those harvested in their entirety, encompassing the endosperm, bran, and germ of the grain. As they undergo minimal processing, they retain a wealth of nutrients, including fiber, vitamins, and minerals. Oats, barley, quinoa, popcorn, and brown rice are examples of whole grains. When selecting carbohydrates, pay attention to the ingredients list on the packaging, look for terms like "whole wheat" or "whole grain." Be wary of claims on the front of the packaging, which may be deceptive.

It's suggested that whole grains should make up at least half of your carbohydrate intake. If you're using the plate method for meal preparation, healthy carbohydrates should occupy a quarter of your plate.

Foods High in Fiber

Fiber is particularly crucial for those with CKD, because as kidney function deteriorates, your body's ability to expel toxins decreases. Fiber contributes to gut health, which can help eliminate some accumulating toxins in your body. A diet low in fiber is associated with increased inflammation and a heightened risk of heart disease. The typical American diet is usually deficient in fiber, which isn't beneficial for overall health. The daily recommended fiber intake is more than 25 grams for women under 50 and over 21 grams for women older than 51. Men under 50 require more than 38 grams of fiber daily and men older than 51 need over 28 grams per day.

Whole grains, fruits, and vegetables are all high in fiber, so make sure to include these beneficial foods in your diet. Some kidney-friendly choices include jicama, eggplant, kale, chickpeas, berries, plums, chia seeds, flaxseed, and whole-grain cereals.

Beneficial Fats

Fats, another macronutrient, have often been negatively perceived. Many have believed that consumption of fats leads to weight gain. However, this isn't true. Fats are necessary nutrients that should account for 20 to 35 percent of your daily calorie intake. They contribute to the normal functioning of the brain and nervous system, regulate cholesterol levels, and reduce inflammation, all crucial for individuals with CKD. When incorporating fats into your diet, it's important to minimize your intake of "bad" fats (saturated and trans fats) and select "good" fats (unsaturated fats).

Saturated fats can be found in hydrogenated oils, animal proteins, cheese, butter, and whole or reduced-fat milk dairy products. Unsaturated fats, on the other hand, are sourced from fatty fish like salmon, walnuts, chia seeds, eggs, olive oil, avocados, avocado oil, and peanut butter.

Using olive or avocado oil for cooking or creating dressings, sauces, and marinades is a good practice. Also, unsalted nut butters or a proper serving of nuts as a snack can be a tasty way to include healthy fats in your diet. Remember, fats are high in calories, so even small quantities can be substantial.

HEALTHY BEGINNINGS: ENJOYABLE BREAKFAST RECIPES TO REJUVENATE YOUR KIDNEYS

Starting your day with a healthy breakfast is a crucial part of a kidney-friendly diet, assisting those with kidney disease to begin their day positively. A well-balanced breakfast can help stabilize blood sugar levels, enhance energy levels, and provide a range of essential nutrients.

When planning a kidney-friendly breakfast, it's crucial to select foods that are low in sodium, potassium, and phosphorus. Suitable choices may include egg whites, low-sodium bread or toast, low-potassium fruits like berries or apples, and non-dairy milk alternatives.

Also, remember to consider portion sizes and avoid high-calorie or high-fat breakfast items, such as bacon or pastries, which can be detrimental to overall health.

SPICY CORN BREAD

Preparation time: 10 minutes

Cooking time: 30 minutes

Servings: 8

Ingredients:

- 1 cup all-purpose white flour
- 1 cup plain cornmeal
- 1 tablespoon sugar
- 2 teaspoon baking powder
- 1 teaspoon chili powder
- 1/4 teaspoon black pepper
- 1 cup rice milk, unenriched
- 1 egg
- 1 egg white
- 2 tablespoon canola oil
- 1/2 cup scallions, finely chopped
- 1/4 cup carrots, finely grated
- 1 garlic clove, minced

Directions:

1. Preheat your oven to 400 degrees f.
2. Start by mixing the flour with baking powder, sugar, cornmeal, pepper and chili powder in a mixing bowl.
3. Stir in oil, milk, egg white, and egg.
4. Mix well until it's smooth, then stir in carrots, garlic, and scallions.
5. Stir well, then spread the batter in an 8-inch baking pan greased with cooking spray.
6. Bake for 30 minutes until golden brown.
7. Slice and serve fresh.

GRANDMA'S PANCAKE SPECIAL

Preparation time: 5 minutes

Cooking time: 15 minutes

Servings: 3

Ingredients:

- 1 tablespoon oil
- 1 cup milk
- 1 egg
- 2 teaspoons sodium-free baking powder
- 4 tablespoons stevia
- 1 ¼ cups flour

Directions:

1. Mix all the dry ingredients, such as flour, stevia, and baking powder.

2. Combine oil, milk, and egg in another bowl. Once done, add them all to the flour mixture.

3. As you stir the mixture, blend them until slightly lumpy.

4. Pour at least ¼ cup of the batter on a hot, greased griddle to make each pancake.

5. Ensure the bottom is brown, then turn and cook the other side.

RASPBERRY OVERNIGHT PORRIDGE

Preparation time: overnight

Cooking time: 0 minute

Servings: 12

Ingredients:

- 1/3 cup rolled oats
- ½ cup almond milk
- 1 tablespoon honey
- 5-6 raspberries, fresh or canned and unsweetened
- 1/3 cup rolled oats
- ½ cup almond milk
- 1 tablespoon honey
- 5-6 raspberries, fresh or canned and unsweetened

Directions:

1. Mix the oats, almond milk, and honey inside a mason jar and place into the fridge overnight.

2. Serve the next morning with the raspberries on top.

MEXICAN STYLE BURRITOS

Preparation time: 5 mins

Cooking time: fifteen mins

Servings: two

Ingredients:

- 1 tablespoon olive oil
- 2 corn tortillas
- ¼ cup, sliced red onion
- ¼ cup, chopped red bell peppers
- ½, deseeded and chopped red chili
- 2 eggs
- Juice of 1 lime
- 1 tablespoon chopped cilantro

Directions:

1 Turn the broiler to medium heat and place the tortillas underneath for 1 to 2 mins on every end or till mildly toasted.
2 Remove and keep the broiler on.
3 Sauté onion, chili and bell peppers for 5 to 6 minutes or until soft.
4 Place the eggs on top of the onions and peppers and place the skillet under the broiler for 5-6 minutes or 'til the eggs are cooked.
5 Serve half the eggs and vegetables on top of each tortilla and sprinkle with cilantro and lime juice to serve.

VANILLA PANCAKES

Preparation time: 15 minutes

Cooking time: 8 minutes

Servings: 2

Ingredients:

- ¼ cup all-purpose white flour
- 1 teaspoon baking powder
- ¼ cup fat-free milk
- 6 egg whites
- 1 tablespoon maple syrup
- 1/8 tsp. organic vanilla extract
- Olive oil cooking spray

Directions:

1. Inside a large-sized container, blend flour and baking powder.
2. Add remaining ingredients and mix until well blended.
3. Preheat the waffle iron then grease it with cooking spray.
4. Place half of the mixture in the preheated waffle iron and cook for approximately 3-4 minutes or until golden brown.
5. Repeat with the remaining mixture.
6. Serve warm.

APPLE OMELET

Preparation time: 10 mins

Cooking time: 8 mins

Servings: two

Ingredients:

- 6 egg whites
- ¼ cup fat-free milk
- one tablespoon water
- Freshly ground black pepper, as required
- 1 tablespoon olive oil
- 1 apple, peeled, cored, and thinly sliced
- ¾ cup onion, thinly sliced
- 2 tablespoons part-skim mozzarella cheese, shredded

Directions:

1. Preheat your oven to 400 °F.
2. In a glass bowl, add egg whites, milk, water, and black pepper and whisk well.
3. In a small-sized ovenproof wok, heat oil over medium heat and sauté apple and onion for approximately 5-6 minutes.
4. With the spatula, spread the apple mixture in the bottom of the wok.
5. Sprinkle with the cheese and top with the egg mixture evenly.
6. Transfer the wok to the oven and bake for approximately 10-12 minutes.
7. Remove the wok from the oven and cut the omelet into 2 equal-sized portions.
8. Serve hot.

FETA MINT OMELET

Preparation time: ten mins

Cooking time: 5 mins

Servings: one

Ingredients:

- 3 eggs
- quarter cup fresh mint, chopped
- 2 tbsp coconut milk
- 1/2 tsp olive oil
- 2 tbsp feta cheese, crumbled
- Pepper
- Salt

Directions:

1. Whisk eggs with feta cheese, mint, milk, pepper, and salt in a bowl.
2. Heat olive oil in a pan over low heat.
3. Pour egg mixture into the pan, then cook until eggs are set.
4. Flip omelet and cook for 2 minutes more.
5. Serve and enjoy.

FRENCH TOAST WITH APPLESAUCE

Preparation time: 5 minutes

Cooking time: 15 minutes

Servings: 6

Ingredients:

- ¼ cup unsweetened applesauce
- ½ cup milk
- 1 teaspoon ground cinnamon
- 2 eggs
- 4 tablespoons stevia
- 6 slices whole wheat bread

Directions:

1. Mix applesauce, stevia, cinnamon, milk, and eggs well in a mixing bowl.
2. Dip the bread into the applesauce mixture until wet; note that you should do this one slice at a time.
3. On medium fire, heat a nonstick skillet greased with cooking spray.
4. Add soaked bread one at a time then cook for 2-3 minutes per side or 'til lightly browned. Serve and enjoy.

FAST MICROWAVE EGG SCRAMBLE

Preparation time: five mins

Cooking time: 1-2 mins

Servings: one

Ingredients:

- 1 large egg
- 2 large egg whites
- 2 tablespoons of milk
- Kosher pepper, ground

Directions:

1 Spray a coffee cup with a bit of cooking spray.
2 Whisk all the ingredients together and place them into the coffee cup.
3 Place the cup with the eggs into the microwave and set to cook for approx. 45 seconds. Take out and stir.
4 Cook it for another 30 seconds after returning it to the microwave.
5 Serve.

BREAKFAST MAPLE SAUSAGE

Preparation time: 15 minutes

Cooking time: 8 minutes

Servings: 12

Ingredients:

- 1 pound of pork, minced
- ½ pound lean turkey meat, ground
- ¼ teaspoon of nutmeg
- ½ teaspoon black pepper
- ¼ all spice
- 2 tablespoons of maple syrup
- 1 tablespoon of water

Directions:

1. Combine all the ingredients in a bowl.
2. Cover and refrigerate for 3-4 hours.
3. Take the mixture and form it into small flat patties with your hand (around 10-12 patties).
4. Mildly oil an average griddle using oil and shallow fry the patties over medium to high heat until brown (around 4-5 minutes on each side).
5. Serve hot.

SUMMER VEGGIE OMELET

Preparation time: 5 minutes

Cooking time: 5 minutes

Servings: 2

Ingredients:

- 4 large egg whites
- ¼ cup of sweet corn, frozen
- 1/3 cup of zucchini, grated
- 2 green onions, sliced
- 1 tablespoon of cream cheese
- Kosher pepper

Directions:

1. Oil a medium pan using cooking spray and include the onions, corn and grated zucchini.
2. Sauté for a couple of minutes until softened.
3. Beat the eggs with water, cream cheese, and pepper in a bowl.
4. Add the eggs to the veggie mixture in the pan, and let cook while moving the edges from inside to outside with a spatula to allow the raw egg to cook through the edges.
5. Turn the omelet with the aid of a dish (placed over the pan, flipped upside down, and then back to the pan).
6. Let sit for another 1-2 minutes.
7. Fold in parts & serve.

PASTA WITH INDIAN LENTILS

Preparation time: five mins

Cooking time: 0 mins

Servings: six

Ingredients:

- ¼-½ cup fresh cilantro (sliced)
- 3 cups water
- two small dry red peppers (whole)
- one teaspoons turmeric
- one tsp. ground cumin
- two to three cloves garlic (crushed)
- one large onion (chopped)
- ½ cup dry lentils (rinsed)
- ½ cup orzo or tiny pasta

Directions:

1. Combine all the ingredients in the skillet except the cilantro, and then boil on moderatehigh flame.
2. Conceal and slightly diminish flame to moderate-low and simmer until pasta is tender for about 35 minutes.
3. Afterward, take out the chili peppers, add cilantro and top it with low-fat sour cream.

CORNMEAL WAFFLES

Preparation time: 15 minutes

Cooking time: 40 minutes

Servings: 8

Ingredients:

- ½ cup warm water
- 2 envelopes of active dry yeast
- 2 cups unsweetened rice milk
- ¼ cup olive oil
- 1 teaspoon white sugar
- 4 egg whites, lightly beaten
- 1 ½ cups all-purpose white flour
- ½ cup cornmeal
- Olive oil cooking spray

Directions:

1. Add warm water and yeast to a large bowl and stir until dissolves completely.
2. Set aside for approximately 5 minutes.
3. Add rice milk, oil, and sugar and whisk until well blended.
4. Add egg whites, flour, and cornmeal and whisk until just moistened.
5. Set the waffle mixture aside in a warm place for approximately 15 minutes.
6. Preheat the waffle iron then grease it with cooking spray.
7. Cook the necessary quantity of the combination inside the waffle iron once it has been warmed for roughly four to five mins.

8   Continue Repeating the process with the leftover portion of
    the solution.
9   Serve warm.

COTTAGE CHEESE PANCAKES

Preparation time: 15 mins

Cooking time: 30 mins

Servings: 6

Ingredients:

- one cup low-fat cottage cheese
- half cup all-purpose white flour sifted
- 1/3 cup unsalted butter, melted
- 8 egg whites, lightly beaten
- Olive oil cooking spray

Directions:

1 In a bowl, add cheese, flour, butter, and eggs and mix until well blended.
2 Lightly grease a non-stick wok using cooking spray and warm over moderate-high flame.
3 Include about ¼ cup of solution and the pot to disperse in an even layer.
4 Cook for approximately 2-3 minutes.
5 Carefully flip the end and cook for roughly one to two mins.
6 Replicate with the rest of the mixture.
7 Serve warm.

BUCKWHEAT AND GRAPEFRUIT PORRIDGE

Preparation time: five mins

Cooking time: 20 mins

Servings: two

Ingredients:

- half cup buckwheat
- ¼, chopped grapefruit
- one tablespoon honey
- one and a half cups almond milk
- 2 cups water

Directions:

1. Boil water on the stove. Add the buckwheat and place the lid on the pan.
2. Simmer for 7 to 10 minutes in low heat. Check to ensure the water does not dry out.
3. Remove and set aside for 5 minutes when most of the water is absorbed.
4. Drain excess water from the pan and stir in almond milk, heating through for 5 minutes.
5. Add the honey and grapefruit.
6. Serve.

AMERICAN BLUEBERRY PANCAKES

Preparation time: 5 minutes

Cooking time: 10 minutes

Servings: 6

Ingredients:

- 1 ½ cups of all-purpose flour, sifted
- 1 cup of oil milk
- 3 tablespoons of sugar
- 2 tablespoons of unsalted oil, melted
- 2 teaspoons of baking powder
- 2 eggs, beaten
- 1 cup of canned blueberries, rinsed

Directions:

1. Combine the baking powder, flour and sugar in a bowl.
2. Make a hole in the center and slowly add the rest of the ingredients.
3. Begin to stir gently from the sides to the center with a spatula until you get a smooth and creamy batter.
4. With cooking spray, spray the pan and place across moderate flame.
5. Take one measuring cup and fill 1/3rd of its capacity with the batter to make each pancake.
6. Use a spoon to pour the pancake batter and cook till golden brown. Wrap once to cook the other end.
7. Serve warm with optional agave syrup.

MEXICAN SCRAMBLED EGGS IN TORTILLA

Preparation time: five mins

Cooking time: 2 mins

Servings: two

Ingredients:

- two medium corn tortillas
- 4 egg whites
- 1 teaspoon of cumin
- 3 teaspoons of green chilies, diced
- ½ teaspoon of hot pepper sauce
- 2 tablespoons of salsa
- ½ teaspoon salt

Directions:

1 Spray some cooking spray on a medium skillet and heat for a few seconds.
2 Whisk the eggs with the green chilies, hot sauce, and comminute 3. Add the eggs to the pan, and whisk with a spatula to scramble. Add the salt.
3 Cook until fluffy and done (1-2 minutes) over low heat.
4 Open the tortillas and spread one tablespoon of salsa on each.
5 Distribute the egg mixture onto the tortillas and wrap gently to make a burrito.
6 Serve warm.

CORNBREAD WITH SOUTHERN TWIST

Preparation time: 15 minutes

Cooking time: 60 minutes

Servings: 8

Ingredients:

- 2 tablespoons shortening
- 1 ¼ cups skim milk
- ¼ cup egg substitute
- 4 tablespoons sodium-free baking powder
- ½ cup flour
- 1 ½ cups cornmeal

Directions:

1 Prepare an 8x8-inch baking dish or a black iron skillet, then add shortening.
2 Put the baking dish or skillet inside the oven at 425 °F; once the shortening has melted, the pan is already hot.
3 In a bowl, add milk and egg, and then mix well.
4 Take out the skillet, add the melted shortening to the batter and stir well.
5 Pour mixture into skillet after mixing all the ingredients.
6 Cook the cornbread for 15-20 minutes until it is golden brown.

BERRIES CHEESE & YOGURT BOWL

Preparation time: 10 minutes

Cooking time: 0 minutes

Servings: 2

Ingredients:

- ½ cup fat-free plain Greek yogurt
- ½ cup low-fat cottage cheese
- 2 teaspoons olive oil
- ¼ teaspoon ground cinnamon
- ¼ cup fresh strawberries, hulled and sliced
- ¼ cup fresh blueberries
- ¼ cup fresh raspberries

Directions:

1. In a large-sized bowl, add the yogurt, cheese, oil, and cinnamon and mix until well blended.
2. Divide the yogurt mixture into 2 serving bowls.
3. Top with berries and serve immediately.

CAULIFLOWER & PEAR PORRIDGE

Preparation time: 10 minutes

Cooking time: 25 minutes

Servings: 6

Ingredients:

- 2 cups pear, peeled, cored, and shredded
- ½ cup low-fat unsweetened coconut, shredded
- ½ cup cauliflower rice
- 1 ¾ cups fat-free milk
- 1 teaspoon organic vanilla extract
- ¾ cup fresh strawberries, hulled and sliced

Directions:

1. In a large-sized saucepan, stir together all ingredients except for strawberries over medium heat and bring it to a gentle boil.

2. Now, reduce the heat to low and simmer for approximately 15-20 minutes.

3. Serve warm with the topping of strawberries.

KIDNEYS-FRIENDLY SNACKS AND APPETIZERS FOR EVERY OCCASION

Healthy nibbling forms a vital part of the kidney-friendly diet, particularly for individuals who might be prone to overeating due to hunger pangs between meals. Snacking can aid in sustaining energy levels, curbing overindulgence during meals, and offering a source of critical nutrients.

However, snack choices should be low in sodium, potassium, and phosphorus. Options might include fresh fruits, vegetables, low-sodium crackers, or a moderate quantity of nuts.

Moreover, regulating portions is crucial when it comes to snacking. It's essential to opt for healthy choices in suitable portion sizes to prevent excessive intake of calories or nutrients that ought to be restricted in the kidney-friendly diet.

ADDICTIVE PRETZELS

Preparation time: 10 minutes

Cooking time: 1 hour

Servings: 6

Ingredients:

- 32-ounce bag of unsalted pretzels
- 1 cup canola oil
- 2 tablespoon seasoning mix
- 3 teaspoon garlic powder
- 3 teaspoons dried dill weed

Directions:

- Warm up the microwave to 175 degrees f.
- Put the pretzels on a cooking sheet and break them into pieces.
- Mix garlic powder and dill in a bowl and reserve half of the mixture.
- Mix the remaining half with seasoning mix and ¾ cup of canola oil.
- Pour this oil over the pretzels and brush them liberally
- Bake the pieces for 1 hour, then flip them to bake for another 15 minutes.
- Allow them to cool, then sprinkle the remaining dill mixture and sprinkle additional oil on surface.
- Serve fresh and warm.

SWEET AND SPICY TORTILLA CHIPS

Preparation time: 10 minutes

Cooking time: 8 minutes

Servings: 6

Ingredients:

- 1/4 cup butter
- 1 teaspoon brown sugar
- 1/2 teaspoon ground chili powder
- 1/2 tsp. garlic powder
- half tsp. ground cumin
- quarter tsp. ground cayenne pepper
- 6 flour tortillas, 6" size

Directions:

- Preheat oven to 425 degrees f.
- Grease a baking sheet with cooking spray.
- Add all spices, brown sugar, and melted butter to a small container.
- Combine thoroughly and put this mixture away.
- Slice the tortillas into eight wedges and brush them with the sugar mixture.
- Spread them on the baking sheet and bake them for 8 mins.
- Serve fresh.

SPICY GUACAMOLE

Preparation time: 15 minutes

Cooking time: 15 minutes

Servings: 4 (about three tablespoons per serving)

Ingredients:

- 1½ tbsps. freshly squeezed lime juice
- one tbsp. minced jalapeño
- pepper, or to taste
- one tbsp. minced red onion
- one tbsp. sliced fresh cilantro
- one garlic clove, crushed
- one-eighth to ¼ tsp. kosher salt
- Freshly ground black pepper

Directions:

1. Mix well with the lime juice, jalapeño, onion, cilantro, garlic, salt, and pepper in a large bowl.

VEGETABLE ROLLS

Preparation time: 30 minutes

Cooking time: 0 minutes

Servings: 8

Ingredients:

- ½ cup finely shredded red cabbage
- ½ cup grated carrot
- ¼ cup julienne red bell pepper
- ¼ cup, both green and white parts julienned scallion
- ¼ cup chopped cilantro
- one tbsp. olive oil
- quarter tsp. ground cumin
- ¼ tsp. freshly ground black pepper
- one sliced very thin strips English cucumber

Directions:

1. In a bowl, toss the black pepper, cumin, olive oil, cilantro, scallion, red pepper, carrot, and cabbage. Mix well.
2. Evenly divide the vegetable filling among the cucumber strips, placing the filling close to one end of the strip.
3. Roll up the cucumber strips around the filling and secure them with a wooden pick.
4. Repeat with each cucumber strip.

SHRIMP SPREAD WITH CRACKERS

Preparation time: 10 minutes

Cooking time: 0 minutes

Servings: 6

Ingredients:

- 1/4 cup light cream cheese
- 2 1/2-ounce cooked, shelled shrimp, minced
- 1 tablespoon of no-salt-added ketchup
- 1/4 teaspoon hot sauce
- 1 teaspoon Worcestershire sauce
- 1/2 teaspoon herb seasoning blend
- 24 matzo cracker miniatures
- 1 tablespoon parsley

Directions:

- Start by tossing the minced shrimp with cream cheese in a bowl.
- Stir in Worcestershire sauce, hot sauce, herb seasoning, and ketchup.
- Mix well and garnish with minced parsley.
- Serve the spread with the crackers.

MANGO CHILLER

Preparation time: 5 minutes

Cooking time: 5 minutes

Servings: 4 (½ cup per serving)

Ingredients:

- 2 cups frozen mango chunks
- ½ cup plain 2% Greek yogurt
- ¼ cup 1% almond milk
- 2 teaspoons honey (optional)

Directions:

- Mix the mango and yogurt in a food processor or blender. Add the almond milk, a bit at a time, to get it to soft ice cream consistency.
- Taste, and add honey if you like. Enjoy instantly.

VEGGIE SNACK

Preparation time: 5 minutes

Cooking time: 10 minutes

Servings: 1

Ingredients:

- 1 large yellow pepper
- 5 carrots
- 5 stalks celery

Directions:

1. Clean the carrots and rinse them under running water.
2. Rinse celery and yellow pepper. Remove the seeds of pepper and chop the veggies into small sticks.
3. Put in a bowl and serve.

BLUEBERRY-RICOTTA SWIRL

Preparation time: five mins

Cooking time: 5 mins

Servings: two

Ingredients:

- half cup fresh or frozen blueberries
- ½ cup part-skim ricotta cheese
- 1 teaspoon sugar
- ½ teaspoon lemon zest (optional)

Directions:

1. If using frozen blueberries, warm them in a saucepan over medium heat until they are thawed but not hot.
2. Meanwhile, mix the sugar with the ricotta in a medium bowl.
3. Mix the blueberries into the ricotta, leaving a few out. Taste, and add more sugar if desired. Top with the remaining blueberries and lemon zest (if using).

HAPPY HEART ENERGY BITES

Preparation time: 20 mins

Cooking time: thirty mins

Servings: Makes 30 (two balls per serving)

Ingredients:

- one cup rolled oats
- three-quarter cup sliced walnuts
- half cup natural peanut butter
- ½ cup ground flaxseed
- ¼ cup honey
- ¼ cup dried cranberries

Directions:

- Inside a huge container, mix the oats, walnuts, peanut butter, flaxseed, honey, and cranberries. Refrigerate for 10 to 20 minutes, if you can, to make them easier to roll.
- Roll into ¾-inch balls. Store in the fridge or freezer if they don't disappear first.

JALAPENO SALSA

Preparation time: 10 minutes

Cooking time: 0 minutes

Servings: 8

Ingredients:

- 4 Roma tomatoes, chopped
- 2 green onions, chopped
- 3 garlic cloves, minced
- one green bell pepper, sliced
- one fresh jalapeño, sliced
- ½ bunch of fresh cilantros, sliced
- ½ teaspoon cumin
- ¼ cup fresh oregano, chopped

Directions:

- Add bell pepper, jalapeno, cilantro, tomatoes, onion, and all other ingredients to a blender.
- Blend this salsa mixture until it gets chunky.
- Serve fresh.

POPCORN WITH SUGAR AND SPICE

Preparation time: 10 minutes

Cooking time: 10 minutes

Servings: 2

Ingredients:

- 8 cups hot popcorn
- 2 tablespoons unsalted butter
- 2 tablespoons sugar
- 1/2 teaspoon cinnamon
- 1/4 teaspoon nutmeg

Directions:

- Popping the corn, put aside.
- Heat the butter, sugar, cinnamon, and nutmeg in the microwave or saucepan over a range fire 'til the butter is melted, and the sugar dissolves.
- Sprinkle the corn with the spicy butter, and mix well.
- Serve immediately for optimal flavor.

PECAN CARAMEL CORN

Preparation time: 10 minutes

Cooking time: 1 hour, 5 minutes

Servings: 10

Ingredients:

- 20 cups popped popcorn
- 2 cups unbranched almonds
- 1 cup pecan halves
- 2 cups stevia
- 1 cup oil
- ½ cup corn syrup
- Pinch cream of tartar
- 1 teaspoon baking soda

Directions:

1 Layer a large roasting pan with popcorn, almonds, and pecans.
2 Cook stevia with corn syrup, oil, and cream of tartar in a heavy saucepan.
3 Stir this syrup for 5 minutes on a boil, then stir in baking soda.
4 Pour this caramel sauce over the popcorn and almonds in the pan.
5 Bake the almonds and popcorn for 1 hour at 200°F in the oven.
6 Stir well, then serve.

SAUTÉED SPICY CABBAGE

Preparation time: 15 minutes

Cooking time: 5 minutes

Servings: 6

Ingredients:

- 3 tablespoons olive oil
- 3 cups chopped green cabbage
- 3 cups chopped red cabbage
- 2 garlic cloves, minced
- 1/8 teaspoon cayenne pepper
- Pinch salt

Directions:

1. Cook olive oil inside a big griddle across moderate flame.
2. Mix in red and green cabbage and the garlic; sauté till the leaves wilt and are tender, about 4 to 5 minutes.
3. Sprinkle the vegetables with the cayenne pepper and salt, toss, and serve.

SPICY CRAB DIP

Preparation time: 10 minutes

Cooking time: 20 minutes

Servings: 1

Ingredients:

- 1 can of 8 oz. softened cream cheese
- 1 tbsp. finely chopped onions
- 1 tbsp. lemon juice
- 2 tbsp. Worcestershire sauce
- 1/8 tsp. black pepper cayenne pepper to taste
- 2 tbsp. to s. of almond milk or non-fortified rice drink
- 1 can of 6 oz. of crabmeat

Directions:

- Preheat the oven to 375 degrees F.
- Pour the cheese cream into a bowl. Add the onions, lemon juice, Worcestershire sauce, black pepper, and cayenne pepper. Mix well. Stir in the almond milk/rice drink.
- Add the crabmeat and mix until you obtain a homogeneous mixture.
- Pour the mixture into a baking dish. Cook without covering for 15 minutes or until bubbles appear. Serve hot with triangle-cut pita bread.
- Microwave until bubbles appear, about 4 minutes, stirring every 1 to 2 minutes.

ROSEMARY AND WHITE BEAN DIP

Preparation time: 10 minutes

Cooking time: 10 minutes

Servings: 10 (¼ cup per serving)

Ingredients:

- 1 (fifteen-oz.) can of cannellini beans, washed & wearied
- two tbsps. additional-virgin olive oil
- 1 garlic clove, peeled
- 1 teaspoon finely chopped fresh rosemary
- Pinch cayenne pepper
- Freshly ground black pepper
- 1 (7.5-ounce) jar marinated artichoke hearts, drained

Directions:

1. Blend the beans, oil, garlic, rosemary, cayenne pepper, and black pepper in a food processor until smooth.
2. Add the artichoke hearts, and pulse until roughly chopped but not puréed.

SALADS AND SOUPS

GROUND BEEF AND RICE SOUP

Preparation time: 15 mins

Cooking time: 40 mins

Servings: 1

Ingredients:

- half lb. extra-lean ground beef
- ½, chopped small sweet onion
- 1 tsp. minced garlic
- 2 cups water
- 1 cup low-sodium beef broth
- ½ cup uncooked long-grain white rice
- 1, chopped celery stalk
- ½ cup, cut into – 1-inch pieces of fresh green beans
- 1 tsp. chopped fresh thyme
- Ground black pepper

Directions:

1. Sauté the ground beef in a pot for 6 minutes or until the beef is completely browned.
2. Drain off the excess fat, then add the onion and garlic to the saucepan.
3. Sauté the vegetables for around three mins or till they are tendered.
4. Add the celery, rice, beef broth, and water.
5. Let it boil, reduce the heat to low, and simmer for 30 minutes or until the rice is tender.
6. Add the green beans and thyme and simmer for 3 minutes.
7. Remove the soup from the heat and top using pepper.

TURKEY & LEMON-GRASS SOUP

Preparation time: 5 minutes

Cooking time: 40 minutes

Servings: 4

Ingredients:

- 1 fresh lime
- ¼ cup fresh basil leaves
- 1 tbsp. cilantro
- 1 cup chestnuts
- 1 tbsp. coconut oil
- 1 thumb-size minced ginger piece
- 2 chopped scallions
- 1 finely chopped green chili
- 4 oz. skinless and sliced turkey breasts
- 1 minced garlic clove, minced
- ½ finely sliced stick of lemon-grass
- 1 chopped white onion, chopped
- 4 cups water

Directions:

1 Crush the lemon grass, cilantro, chili, 1 tbsp oil and basil leaves in a blender or pestle and mortar to form a paste.
2 Heat a large pan/wok with 1 tbsp olive oil.
3 Sauté the onions, garlic and ginger until soft.
4 Add the turkey and brown each side for 4-5 minutes.
5 Add the broth and stir.
6 Now add the paste and stir.
7 Next, add the chestnuts, cool the flame slightly, and simmer for 25-30 mins or till the turkey is thoroughly cooked.
8 Serve hot with the green onion sprinkled over the top.

GREEN BEAN VEGGIE STEW

Preparation time: 10 minutes

Cooking time: 30-35 minutes

Servings: 1

Ingredients:

- 6 cups shredded green cabbage
- 3 celery stalks, chopped
- 1 teaspoon oil
- ½ large sweet onion, chopped
- 1 teaspoon minced garlic
- 1 scallion, chopped
- 2 tablespoons chopped fresh parsley
- 2 tablespoons lemon juice
- 1 teaspoon chopped fresh oregano
- 1 tablespoon chopped fresh thyme
- 1 teaspoon chopped savory
- Water
- 1 cup fresh green beans, cut into 1" pieces
- Black pepper (ground), to taste

Directions:

1. Take a medium-big cooking pan and warm oil across moderate heat.
2. Include onion and stir-cook till it becomes translucent and tender.
3. Add garlic and stir-cook until it becomes fragrant.

4   Add cabbage, celery, scallion, parsley, lemon juice, thyme, savory, and oregano; add water to cover veggies by 3-4 inches.

5   Stir the mixture and boil it.

6   Over low heat, cover and simmer the mixture for about 25 minutes until the veggies are tender.

7   Add green beans and cook for 2-3 more minutes. Season with black pepp, as required. Serve warm.

TUNA MACARONI SALAD

Preparation time: 5 minutes

Cooking time: 25 minutes

Servings: 10 servings

Ingredients:

- 1 1/2 cups uncooked macaroni
- 1 (6 oz.) can of tuna in water
- 1/4 cup mayonnaise
- 2 medium celery stalks, diced
- 1 tbsp. lemon pepper seasoning

Directions:

1. Cook the pasta and let it cool in the refrigerator.
2. Drain the tuna in a colander and rinse it with cold water.
3. Add the tuna and celery once the macaroni has cooled.
4. Stir in mayonnaise and sprinkle with lemon seasoning. Mix well. Serve cold.

WILD RICE ASPARAGUS SOUP

Preparation time: 10 minutes

Cooking time: 30 minutes

Servings: 4

Ingredients:

- 3/4 cup wild rice
- 2 cups asparagus, chopped
- 1 cup carrots, diced
- 1/2 cup onion, diced
- 3 garlic cloves, minced
- 1/4 cup oil
- 1/2 tsp thyme
- 1/2 tsp fresh ground pepper
- 1/4 tsp nutmeg
- 1 bay leaf
- 1/2 cup all-purpose flour
- 4 cups low-sodium chicken broth
- half cup extra dry vermouth
- two cups cooked chicken
- cups unsweetened almond milk, unenriched

Directions:

1. Cook the wild rice as per the cooking instructions on the box or bag and drain.
2. Melt the oil inside a Dutch oven and fry garlic and onion.
3. Once soft, add spices, herbs, and carrots.
4. Cook on medium heat until veggies are tender, then add flour and stir; cook for 10 minutes on low heat.

5   Add 4 cups of broth and vermouth and blend using a handheld blender.

6   Dice the chicken pieces and add asparagus and chicken to the soup.

7   Mix in almond milk and cook for 20 mins.

8   Include the wild rice and serve warm.

BUTTERSCOTCH APPLE SALAD

Preparation time: 5 minutes

Cooking time: 0 minutes

Servings: 6

Ingredients:

- 3 cups jazz apples, chopped
- 8 oz. canned crushed pineapple
- 8 oz. whipped topping
- 1/2 cup butterscotch topping
- 1/3 cup almonds
- 1/4 cup butterscotch

Directions:

1. Place the entire salad components into a suitable salad container.
2. Whisk them thoroughly and refrigerate for 1 hour.
3. Serve.

CHESTNUT NOODLE SALAD

Preparation time: 5 minutes

Cooking time: 0 minutes

Servings: 6

Ingredients:

- 8 cups cabbage, shredded
- 1/2 cup canned chestnuts, sliced
- 6 green onions, chopped
- 1/4 cup olive oil
- 1/4 cup apple cider vinegar
- 3/4 teaspoon stevia
- 1/8 teaspoon black pepper
- 1 cup chow Mein noodles, cooked

Directions:

1. Take a suitable salad bowl.

2. Start tossing in all the ingredients.

3. Mix well and serve.

PAPRIKA PORK SOUP

Preparation time: 5 minutes

Cooking time: 35 minutes

Servings: 2

Ingredients:

- 4-ounce sliced pork loin
- 1 teaspoon black pepper
- 2 minced garlic cloves
- 3 cups water
- 1 tablespoon extra-virgin olive oil
- 1 chopped onion
- 1 tablespoon paprika

Directions:

1　Add in the oil, chopped onion and minced garlic.
2　Sauté for 5 minutes on low heat.
3　Add the pork slices to the onions and cook for 7-8 mins or till browned.
4　Include the water to the pan and raise towards a boil on high flame.
5　Diminish flame then simmer for twenty mins or until pork is thoroughly cooked.
6　Season with pepper to serve.

BEEF OKRA SOUP

Preparation time: 10 minutes

Cooking time: 45-55 minutes

Servings: 1

Ingredients:

- ½ cup okra
- ½ teaspoon basil
- ½ cup carrots, diced
- ½ cups water
- 1-pound beef stew meat
- 1 cup raw sliced onions
- ½ cup green peas
- 1 teaspoon black pepper
- ½ teaspoon thyme
- ½ cup corn kernels

Directions:

1 Take a medium-large cooking pot and heat oil over medium heat.
2 Add water, beef stew meat, black pepper, onions, basil, thyme, and stir-cook for 40-45 minutes until meat is tender.
3 Add all veggies. Over low heat, simmer the mixture for about 20-25 minutes. Add more water if needed.
4 Serve soup warm.

CHICKEN WILD RICE SOUP

Preparation time: 10 minutes

Cooking time: 15 minutes

Servings: 6

Ingredients:

- 2/3 cup wild rice, uncooked
- tbsp onion, chopped finely
- 1 tbsp fresh parsley, chopped
- 1 cup carrots, chopped
- 8 oz chicken breast, cooked
- 2 tbsp oil
- 1/4 cup all-purpose white flour
- 5 cups low-sodium chicken broth
- 1 tbsp slivered almonds

Directions:

1. Start by adding rice and 2 cups broth, and ½ cup water to a cooking pot.
2. Cook 'til the rice is al dente and set it aside.
3. Add oil to a saucepan and melt it.
4. Stir in onion and sauté until soft, then add the flour and the remaining broth.
5. Stir and cook for 1 minute, then add the chicken, cooked rice, and carrots.
6. Cook for 5 minutes on simmer.
7. Garnish with almonds. Serve fresh.

KOREAN PEAR SALAD

Preparation time: 5 minutes

Cooking time: 15 minutes

Servings: 2

Ingredients:

- 6 cups green lettuce
- 4 medium-sized pears (peeled, cored, and diced)
- ½ cup sugar
- half cup pecan nuts
- ½ cup water two oz blue cheese
- ½ cup of cranberries
- ½ cup of dressing

Directions:

1 Dissolve the water and sugar in a frying pan (non-stick).
2 Heat the mixture until it turns into syrup, and then add the nuts immediately.
3 Place the syrup on parchment paper and separate the nuts while the mixture is hot. Let it cool down.
4 Prepare lettuce inside a salad container and include the pears, blue cheese, and cranberries to the salad.
5 Add the caramelized nuts to the salad and serve it with a dressing of choice on the end.

GRATED CARROT SALAD WITH LEMON-DIJON VINAIGRETTE

Preparation time: 15 mins

Cooking time: 10 mins

Servings: 8 servings

Ingredients:

- 9 small carrots (5.5"), peeled
- 2 tbsp. 1/2 teaspoon Dijon mustard
- 1 c. lemon juice
- 2 tbsp. extra virgin olive oil
- 1-2 tsp. honey (to taste)
- ¼ tsp. salt
- ¼ tsp. freshly ground pepper (as required)
- two tbsp. sliced parsley
- one green onion, thinly sliced

Directions:

1. Grate the carrots in a food processor.

2. Mix Dijon mustard, lemon juice, honey, olive oil, salt, and pepper inside a salad container. Include the carrots, fresh parsley, and green onions. Mix to seal well. Enclose and refrigerate until ready to be served.

CABBAGE TURKEY SOUP

Preparation time: 10 minutes

Cooking time: 40-45 minutes

Servings: 1

Ingredients:

- ½ cup shredded green cabbage
- ½ cup bulgur
- 2 dried bay leaves
- 2 tablespoons chopped fresh parsley
- 1 teaspoon chopped fresh sage
- 1 teaspoon chopped fresh thyme
- 1 celery stalk, chopped
- 1 carrot, sliced thin
- ½ sweet onion, chopped
- 1 teaspoon minced garlic
- 1 teaspoon olive oil
- ½ pound cooked ground turkey, 93% lean
- 4 cups water
- 1 cup chicken stock
- Pinch red pepper flakes
- Black pepper (ground), to taste

Directions:

1. Take a large saucepan or cooking pot, and add oil. Heat over medium heat.
2. Add turkey and stir-cook for 4-5 minutes until evenly brown.
3. Include onion and garlic, and fry for about three mins to soften the veggies.

4   Add water, chicken stock, cabbage, bulgur, celery, carrot, and bay leaves.

5   Boil the mixture.

6   Over low heat, cover and simmer the mixture for about 30-35 minutes until the bulgur is cooked well and tender.

7   Remove bay leaves. Add parsley, sage, thyme, and red pepper flakes; stir the mixture and top using black pepper. Serve warm.

GREEN TUNA
SALAD

Preparation time: ten mins

Cooking time: fifteen to twenty mins

Servings: two

Ingredients:

- 5 ounces of tuna (in freshwater only)
- 2-3 cups of lettuce
- 1 cup of baby marrow
- 1/2 cup of red bell pepper
- 1/4 cup of red onion
- 1/4 cup of fresh thyme
- 2 tbsp olive oil
- 1/8 tsp of black pepper
- 2 tbsp of red wine vinegar

Directions:

1. Slice the bell pepper, onion, baby marrow, and thyme into small pieces.
2. Add a 3/4 cup of water to a saucepan and add the bell pepper, onion, baby marrow, and thyme to the pan. Let it boil, and steam the vegetables by adding a lid on top of the saucepan—steam for 10 minutes.
3. Remove the vegetables and drain them.
4. Combine the vegetables (once cooled down) with the chopped tomatoes and tuna.
5. Mix olive oil, red wine vinegar, and black pepper to create a salad dressing.

6   Add the mixture to a bed of lettuce and drizzle the dressing
    on top.

ARLECCHINO RICE SALAD

Preparation time: ten mins

Cooking time: 15 mins

Servings: 3

Ingredients:

- half cup white rice, dried
- one cup chicken stock
- 1 zucchini, shredded
- 2 tbsp. capers
- 1 carrot, shredded
- 1 tomato, chopped
- 1 tbsp. apple cider vinegar
- 1/2 tsp. salt
- 2 tbsp. fresh parsley, chopped
- 1 tbsp. canola oil

Directions:

1. Put rice in the pan.
2. Add chicken stock and boil it with the closed lid for 15–20 minutes or until rice absorbs all water.
3. Meanwhile, combine shredded zucchini, capers, carrot, and tomato in a mixing bowl. Add fresh parsley.
4. Make the dressing: mix the canola oil, salt, and apple cider vinegar.
5. Chill the cooked rice a little and add it in the salad bowl to the vegetables. Add dressing and mix up salad well.

GRILLED CORN ON THE COB

Preparation time: 5 minutes.

Cooking time: 20 minutes.

Servings: 4

Ingredients:

- 4 frozen corn on the cob, cut in half
- 1/2 tsp. thyme
- 1 tbsp. grated parmesan cheese
- 1/4 tsp. black pepper
- Oil for greasing

Directions:

1 Combine the oil, cheese, thyme, and black pepper in a bowl. Place the corn in the cheese/oil mix and roll to coat evenly.
2 Fold all 4 pieces in aluminum foil, leaving a small open surface on top. Place the wrapped corns over the grill and let cook for twenty mins.
3 Serve hot.

PORK MEATLOAF

Preparation time: 10 minutes.

Cooking time: 50 minutes.

Servings: 1

Ingredients:

- 1 lb. lean ground beef
- 1/2 cup breadcrumbs
- 1/2 cup chopped sweet onion
- 1 egg
- 2 tbsps. chopped fresh basil
- 1 tsp. chopped fresh thyme
- 1 tsp. chopped fresh parsley
- 1/4 tsp. ground black pepper
- 1 tbsp. brown sugar
- 1 tsp. white vinegar
- 1/4 tsp. garlic powder

Directions:

1. Preheat the oven to 350°F.
2. Mix the breadcrumbs, beef, onion, basil, egg, thyme, parsley, and pepper well.
3. Stir the brown sugar, vinegar, and garlic powder in a small bowl.
4. Put the brown sugar mixture evenly over the meat.
5. Bake the meatloaf for around 50 mins or till it is cooked thoroughly. Let the meatloaf stand for 10 minutes, and then pour out any accumulated grease.

LEMON POPS

Preparation time: 5 minutes

Cooking time: 5 minutes

Servings: 1

Ingredients:

- 4 tablespoons fresh lemon juice
- Powdered stevia

Directions:

1 Mix mango or lemon juice and stevia and pour into molds.
2 Freeze until firm.

CILANTRO FLOUNDER

Preparation time: twenty mins

Cooking time: 5 mins

Servings: 4

Ingredients:

- quarter cup homemade mayonnaise
- Juice of one lime
- 4 Zest of 1 lime
- ½ cup chopped fresh cilantro
- (3-ounce) flounder fillets
- Ground black pepper

Directions:

1. Warm up the microwave to 400°F. In a bowl, stir simultaneously the cilantro, juice, lime zest, and mayonnaise.
2. Place four pieces of foil, about 8 by 8 inches square, on a clean surface.
3. Place a flounder fillet in the center of every square.
4. Top the fillets evenly with the mayonnaise mixture.
5. Season the flounder with pepper.
6. Wrap the foil's edges across the fish, make a cozy package, and put the foil packets onto a baking tray.
7. Bake the fish for 4 to five minutes.
8. Unfold the packets and serve.

PUMPKIN BITES

Preparation time: 10 minutes.

Cooking time: 5 minutes.

Servings: 12

Ingredients:

- 8 oz. cream cheese
- 1 tsp. vanilla
- 1 tsp. pumpkin pie spice
- 1/4 cup coconut flour
- 1/4 cup erythritol
- 1/2 cup pumpkin puree
- 4 oz. butter

Directions:

1. Add all the ingredients into the mixing bowl and beat using a hand mixer until well combined.
2. Scoop mixture into the silicone ice cube tray and put it inside the fridge till established.
3. Serve & relish.

BEEF KABOBS WITH PEPPER

Preparation time: 5 minutes.

Cooking time: 10 minutes.

Servings: 8

Ingredients:

- 1 lb. beef sirloin
- 1/2 cup vinegar
- 2 tbsp. salad oil
- 1 medium, chopped onion
- 2 tbsp. chopped fresh parsley
- 1/4 tsp. black pepper
- 2 cut into strips green peppers

Directions:

1   Trim the fat from the meat; then cut it into cubes of 1 and 1/2 inches each. Mix vinegar, oil, onion, parsley, and pepper in a bowl,
2   Place the meat in the marinade and set it aside for about 2 hours; make sure to stir from time to time.
3   Remove the meat from the marinade and alternate it on skewers instead with green pepper.
4   Brush the pepper with the marinade and broil for about 10 minutes 4 inches from the heat. Serve and enjoy your kabobs.

CHICKEN BREASTS WITH HERBS

Preparation time: ten mins

Cooking time: thirty mins

Servings: four

Ingredients:

- one-lb. boneless, skinless chicken breasts
- 2 tablespoons garlic and herb seasoning blend
- one tsp. ground black pepper
- one medium onion
- one to two garlic cloves
- ¼ cup olive oil

Directions

1   : Marinating:
2   Chop onion and garlic and place in a bowl. Add Mrs. Dash Seasoning, ground pepper, and olive oil.
3   Add chicken breasts to the marinade then cover it, and refrigerate for at least 4 hours or overnight.
4   Baking:
5   Preheat the oven to 350°F.
6   Cover a baking sheet with foil, place the marinated chicken breasts on the pan.
7   Pour the remaining marinade across the chicken and bake at 350°F for twenty mins.
8   Broil a further five mins for browning.

ONE-POT BEEF ROAST

Preparation time: 10 minutes.

Cooking time: 75 minutes.

Servings: 4

Ingredients:

- 3 (1/2) lb. beef roast
- 4 oz. mushrooms, sliced
- 12 oz. beef stock
- 1-oz. onion soup mix
- 1/2 cup Italian dressing

Directions:

1. Take a bowl and add the stock, onion soup mix, and Italian dressing. Stir.
2. Put beef roast in the pan. Add the mushrooms and stock mix to the pan and cover with foil
3. Preheat your oven to 300°F. Bake for 1 hour and 15 minutes
4. Let the roast cool. Slice and serve. Enjoy the gravy on top!

SALAD AL TONNO

Preparation time: 15 minutes.

Cooking time: 0 minutes.

Servings: 2

Ingredients:

- 1 1/2 cup lettuce leaves, torn
- 1/2 cup cherry red bell peppers, halved
- 1/2 tsp. garlic powder
- 1/2 tsp. salt
- 1/2 tsp. ground black pepper
- 1 tbsp. lemon juice
- 6 oz. tuna, canned, drained

Directions:

1. Chop the tuna roughly and put it in the salad bowl.
2. Add cherry Red bell peppers, lettuce leaves, salt, garlic powder, ground black pepper, lemon juice, and olive oil.
3. Give a good shake to the salad.
4. Salad could be stocked in the refrigerator for around 3 hrs.

SPICY CHICKEN

Preparation time: ten mins

Cooking time: ten mins

Servings: 4

Ingredients:

- half tsp. paprika
- one-eighth tsp. ground white pepper
- ⅛ tsp. onion powder
- ⅛ tsp. salt
- ¼ tsp. cayenne pepper
- quarter tsp. ground cumin
- quarter tsp. dried thyme
- 2 chicken breasts, boneless and skinless

Directions:

1. Warm up your microwave to 350 degrees Fahrenheit.
2. Coat a baking tray with cooking spray.
3. Bring a cast-iron griddle up to a high temperature and set it aside.
4. After adding the oil, cook the mixture for five mins, or till it reaches a smoking point.
5. Inside a low-volume container, combine the following seasonings: salt, paprika, cumin, white pepper, cayenne, thyme, and onion powder.
6. Cover each end of the chicken breast with oil, then roll it in the spice mixture to evenly distribute it.
7. Move the chicken to the heated pot, and cook it for one min on each end.
8. Spread the mixture to the baking sheet you have created and bake for another five mins.

LOW-SODIUM POUND CAKE

Preparation time: 10 minutes

Cooking time: 30 minutes

Servings: 1

Ingredients:

- 1 ¼ cup bread flour
- ¼-lb. butter, unsalted
- ¾ cup sugar or sugar replacement
- 2 large eggs, beaten
- 3 oz. non-fat milk or milk alternative

Directions:

1. Warm up your microwave to 375°F. Prepare a pan by lining an 18-inch x 13-inch pan with baking paper.
2. Cream butter gradually adds sugar and beat until fluffy.
3. Add eggs, milk, and flour and mix well.
4. Pour mixture into the lined pan and bake at 375°F for approximately 30 minutes.

SALMON SALAD

Preparation time: five mins

Cooking time: fifteen mins

Servings: two

Ingredients:

For the Pesto:

- one minced garlic clove
- ½ cup fresh arugula
- ¼ cup additional-virgin olive oil
- half cup fresh basil
- one tbsp. black pepper

For the Salmon:

- 4 ounces skinless salmon fillet
- 1 tablespoon. coconut oil

For the Salad:

- ½ juiced lemon
- 2 sliced radishes
- ½ cup iceberg lettuce
- 1 tablespoon black pepper

Directions:

1 Prepare the pesto by blending all the pesto Ingredients in a kitchen appliance or by grinding with a pestle and mortar. Set aside.

2   Add a skillet to the stove on medium-high heat and melt the copra oil.
3   Add the salmon to the pan.
4   Cook for 7-8 mins and switch across.
5   Cook for an extra 3-4 minutes or until it's well cooked.
6   Eliminate the fillets from the griddle and permit them to rest.
7   Mix the lettuce and therefore the radishes and squeeze over the juice of ½ lemon.
8   Flake the salmon with a fork and blend through the salad.
9   Toss to coat and sprinkle with a little black pepper to serve.

COUSCOUS WITH VEGGIES

Preparation time: 10 mins

Cooking time: 10 mins

Servings: 5

Ingredients:

- half cup uncooked couscous
- 1/4 cup white mushrooms, sliced
- half cup red onion, sliced
- one garlic clove, minced
- half cup frozen peas
- 2 tbsp. dry white wine
- 1/2 tsp. basil
- 2 tbsp. fresh parsley, chopped
- 1 cup water or vegetable stock
- 1 tbsp. margarine or vegetable oil

Directions:

1. Thaw the peas by setting them aside for 15–20 minutes at room temperature. In a medium pan, heat the margarine or vegetable oil.
2. Add onions, peas, mushroom, and garlic and sauté for around 5 minutes. Add the wine and let it evaporate.
3. Add all the herbs and spices and toss well. Take off the heat and keep it aside.
4. In a small pot, cook the couscous with 1 cup of hot water or vegetable stock. Bring to a boil, take off the flame, and sit for a couple of mins with a lid covered. Add the sauté veggies to the couscous and toss well. Serve in a serving bowl, warm or cold.

BEEF CHILI

Preparation time: 10 mins

Cooking time: thirty mins

Servings: two

Ingredients:

- one onion, diced
- one red bell pepper, diced
- 2 cloves garlic, minced
- 6 ounces lean ground beef
- 1 tablespoon chili powder
- 1 tablespoon oregano
- two tbsps. additional-virgin olive oil
- one cup water
- one cup brown rice
- 1 tablespoon fresh cilantro to serve

Directions:

1. Soak vegetables in warm water.
2. Raise a pot of water to a boil then include rice for twenty mins.
3. Meanwhile, add the oil to a pan and warmth on moderate-high flame.
4. Include the pepper, onions, and garlic and fry for five mins until soft.
5. Remove and put aside.
6. Add the meat to the pan and stir until browned.
7. Add the vegetables back to the pan and stir.
8. Now add the favorer and herbs and therefore the water. Cover and switch the warmth down a little to simmer for a quarter-hour.

9   Meanwhile, drain the rice from the rice and the lid and steam while the chili is cooking.

10 Serve hot with the fresh cilantro sprinkled over the highest.

SAUTÉED CHICKPEA AND LENTIL MIX

Preparation time: 10 minutes.

Cooking time: 50 minutes.

Servings: 4

Ingredients:

- 1 cup chickpeas, half-cooked
- 1 cup lentils
- 5 cups chicken stock
- 1/2 cup fresh cilantro, chopped
- 1 tsp. salt
- 1/2 tsp. chili flakes
- 1/4 cup onion, diced
- 1 tbsp. tomato paste

Directions:

1. Place chickpeas in the pan. Add water, salt, and chili flakes.
2. Boil the chickpeas for 30 minutes over medium heat. Then add diced onion, lentils, and tomato paste. Stir well.
3. Close the lid and cook the mix for 15 minutes. After this, add chopped cilantro, stir the meal well and cook it for 5 more minutes. Let the cooked lunch chill a little before serving.

SIMPLE LAMB CHOPS

Preparation time: 35 minutes

Cooking time: 5 minutes

Servings: 3

Ingredients:

- 8 lamb rib chops
- 1 tablespoon garlic, minced
- ¼ cup olive oil
- quarter cup mint, fresh & sliced
- one tbsp. rosemary, fresh & sliced

Directions:

1 Place the rosemary, garlic, mint, and olive oil within a container and thoroughly combine the ingredients.
2 Put a spoonful of the combination aside on the edge in case you need it afterwards.
3 Marinate the lamb slices for half an hour after tossing them in the marinade and allowing them sit there.
4 Get a pan made of cast iron and put it on the stove around moderate-high flame.
5 After adding the lamb, grill it for two mins on each end to achieve a moderate-rare doneness.
6 After the lamb has rested for a couple of mins, sprinkle it with any marinade that is left over.
7 Serve, and have fun with it!

EGGPLANT AND RED PEPPER SOUP

Preparation time: twenty mins

Cooking time: forty mins

Servings: 1

Ingredients:

- one small, cut into quarters sweet onion
- 2 halved small red bell peppers
- 2 cups cubed eggplant
- 1 cloves, crushed garlic
- 1 tbsp. olive oil
- one cup chicken stock Water
- quarter cup sliced fresh basil
- Ground black pepper

Directions:

1. Warm up the microwave to 350°F.
2. Put the onions, red peppers, eggplant, and garlic in a baking dish.
3. Drizzle the vegetables with olive oil; cook vegetables for 30 mins or till they are mildly charred & tender.
4. Cool the vegetables mildly and remove the skin from the peppers. Puree the vegetables with a hand mixer (with the chicken stock).
5. Transfer the soup to a medium pan and include enough water to reach the anticipated depth.
6. Warm the soup to a simmer and include the basil. Season with pepper and serve.

CABBAGE AND BEEF FRY

Preparation time: 5 minutes.

Cooking time: 15 minutes.

Servings: 4

Ingredients:

- 1 lb. beef, ground
- 1/2 lb. bacon
- 1 onion
- 1 garlic clove, minced
- 1/2 head cabbage
- Salt and pepper to taste

Directions:

1. Take a skillet and place it over medium heat. Add chopped bacon, beef, and onion until slightly browned
2. Transfer to a bowl and keep it covered.
3. Add minced garlic and cabbage to the skillet and cook until slightly browned.
4. Return the ground beef mixture to the skillet then simmer over low flame for three to five mins. Serve & relish!

BAKED PORK CHOPS

Preparation time: 15 minutes.

Cooking time: 40 minutes.

Servings: 6

Ingredients:

- 1/2 cup flour
- 1 large egg
- 1/4 cup water
- 3/4 cup breadcrumbs
- 6 (3 1/2 oz.) pork chops
- 2 tbsp. butter, unsalted
- 1 tsp. paprika

Directions:

1. Begin by switching the oven to 350°F to preheat. Mix and spread the flour on a shallow plate. Whisk the egg with water in another shallow bowl. Spread the breadcrumbs on a separate plate.
2. Firstly, coat the pork with flour, then dip in the egg mix and then in the crumbs. Oil a baking tray and put the chops in it. Drizzle the pepper on top and bake for 40 mins. Serve.

DOLMAS WRAP

Preparation time: ten mins.

Cooking time: 5 mins.

Servings: 2

Ingredients:

- two whole-wheat wraps
- 6 dolmas (stuffed grape leaves)
- 1 tomato, chopped
- 1 cucumber, chopped
- 2 oz. Greek yogurt
- 1/2 tsp. minced garlic
- 1/4 cup lettuce, chopped
- 2 oz. feta, crumbled

Directions:

1 Combine chopped tomato, cucumber, Greek yogurt, minced garlic, lettuce, and feta in the mixing bowl.
2 When the mixture is homogenous, transfer it to the center of every wheat wrap.
3 Arrange dolma over the vegetable mixture.
4 Carefully wrap the wheat wraps.

GREEN PALAK PANEER

Preparation time: 5 minutes.

Cooking time: 10 minutes.

Servings: 4

Ingredients:

- 1 lb. green lettuce
- 2 cups cubed paneer (vegan)
- 2 tbsp. coconut oil
- 1 tsp. cumin
- 1 onion, chopped
- 1–2 tsp. hot green chili minced up
- 1 tsp. minced garlic
- 15 cashews
- 15 tbsp. almond milk
- 1 tsp. garam masala
- Flavored vinegar as required Ginger

Directions:

1. Include cashews & almond milk to a mixer and blend well.
2. Set your pot to Sauté mode and add coconut oil; allow the oil to heat up.
3. Add cumin seeds, garlic, green chilies, ginger, and sauté for 1 minute.
4. Add onion and sauté for 2 minutes. Add chopped green lettuce, flavored vinegar, and a cup of water. Lock up the lid and cook at high pressure for 10 minutes. Quick-release the pressure.
5. Include half cup of water and blend to a paste. Include cashew paste, paneer, and Garam Masala and stir thoroughly.

ROSEMARY LAMB

Preparation time: 10 minutes

Cooking time: 6 hours

Servings: 4

Ingredients:

- 2 pounds lamb shoulder, cubed
- 1 tbsp rosemary, chopped
- 3 garlic cloves, minced
- ½ cup lamb stock
- 4 bay leaves
- Salt and black pepper to the taste

Directions:

1 In your slow cooker, combine the lamb with the rosemary and the rest of the ingredients.
2 Put the lid on then cook on High for 6 hours.
3 Divide the mixture among the palates and serve.

CRUSTY SALMON

Preparation time: ten mins

Cooking time: 2 hours

Servings: two

Ingredients:

- 8 ounces salmon fillet
- 2 tablespoons panko bread crumbs
- one-ounce parmesan, aggravated
- one teaspoon dried oregano
- one tsp. sunflower oil

Directions:

1 In the mixing bowl combine together panko breadcrumbs, Parmesan, and dried oregano.
2 Sprinkle the salmon with olive oil and coat it in the breadcrumb's mixture.
3 After this, line the baking tray with baking paper.
4 Place the salmon in the tray and transfer it to the preheated to 385°F oven.
5 Bake the salmon for 25 minutes.

PERSIAN CHICKEN

Preparation time: ten mins.

Cooking time: twenty mins.

Servings: 5

Ingredients:

- half chopped sweet onion
- quarter cup lemon juice
- one tbsp. dried oregano
- one tsp. minced garlic
- 1 tsp. sweet paprika
- half tsp. ground cumin
- half cup olive oil
- 5 boneless, skinless chicken thighs

Directions:

1. Place the cumin, paprika, garlic, oregano, lemon juice, and onion in a food processor and pulse to mix the ingredients.
2. Put olive oil until the mixture is smooth.
3. Put chicken thighs in a large Ziploc and add the marinade for 2 hours.
4. Remove the thighs from the marinade.
5. Preheat the barbecue to moderate. Grill the chicken for about twenty mins, flipping once till it reaches 165°F.

EASY EGG SALAD

Preparation time: five mins.

Cooking time: 8 mins.

Servings: 4

Ingredients:

- 4 large eggs
- half cup sweet onion, chopped
- quarter cup celery, chopped
- one tbsp. yellow mustard
- 1 tsp. smoked paprika
- 3 tbsp. mayo

Directions:

1. Hard-boil the eggs in a small pot filled with water for approx. 7–8 minutes. Leave the eggs in the water for an extra couple of minutes before peeling.
2. Peel the eggs and chop finely with a knife or tool. Combine all the chopped veggies with mayo and mustard. Add in the eggs and combine thoroughly.
3. Drizzle via some smoked paprika on top. Serve cold with pitta, white bread slices, or lettuce wraps.

SUN-DRIED TOMATO PENNE

Preparation time: 20 mins

Cooking time: 10 mins

Servings: four

Ingredients:

- 8 oz. penne
- ½ cup sun-dried tomatoes, drained well
- 2 tbsps. olive oil
- 4 garlic cloves, minced
- 2 tbsps. lemon juice
- 2 tbsps. pine nuts
- 2 tbsps. grated parmesan cheese
- 1 pinch chili flakes

Directions:

1. Cook the penne inside a huge pan of salted water for 8 mins or the time indicated on the package, just until al dente. Drain the penne well.
2. For the pesto, mix the rest of the components inside a blender and mix till well blended and uniform.
3. Mix the pesto with the penne and serve instantly.

MEXICAN CHORIZO SAUSAGE

Preparation time: 10 minutes.

Cooking time: 15 minutes.

Servings: 1

Ingredients:

- 2 lb. boneless pork but coarsely ground
- 3 tbsp. red wine vinegar
- two tbsp. smoked paprika
- half tsp. cinnamon
- 1/2 tsp. ground cloves
- 1/4 tsp. coriander seeds
- 1/4 tsp. ground ginger
- 1 tsp. ground cumin
- 3 tbsp. brandy

Directions:

1. Inside a huge mixing bowl, mix the ground pork with the seasonings, brandy, and vinegar and mix with your hands thoroughly.
2. Put the mixture into a large Ziploc bag and leave it in the fridge overnight. Form into 15– 16 patties of equal size.
3. Heat the oil inside a large pot and fry the patties for 5–7 mins on every end, or until the meat inside is no longer pink, and there is a light brown crust on top.
4. Serve hot.

CALIFORNIA PORK CHOPS

Preparation time: 10 mins.

Cooking time: 10 mins.

Servings: two

Ingredients:

- 1 tablespoon fresh cilantro, chopped
- half cup chives, sliced
- 2 large green bell peppers, chopped
- 1 lb. 1" thick boneless pork chops
- 1 tbsp. fresh lime juice
- 2 cups cooked rice
- 1/8 tsp. dried oregano leaves
- 1/4 tsp. ground black pepper
- 1/4 tsp. ground cumin
- 1 tbsp. butter
- 1 lime

Directions:

1. Start by seasoning the pork chops with lime juice and cilantro.
2. Place them in a shallow dish.
3. Toss the chives with pepper, cumin, butter, oregano, and rice in a bowl.
4. Stuff the bell peppers with this mixture and place them around the pork chops.
5. Cover the chop and bell peppers with a foil sheet and bake them for 10 minutes in the oven at 375°F. Serve warm.

CHIVES DUCK

Preparation time: 20 minutes

Cooking time: 20 minutes

Servings: 4

Ingredients:

- 4 duck breasts, boneless and skin scored
- salt and black pepper to the taste
- 3 tbsp chives, chopped
- 2 tbsp parsley, chopped
- 1 tbsp olive oil
- 3 tbsps. balsamic vinegar
- 1 tsp cinnamon powder
- ½ cup chicken broth
- 2 red onions, chopped

Directions:

1. Heat a skillet with the oil over medium-high heat, add the duck skin side down and cook for 5 minutes.
2. Add the cinnamon and the rest of the ingredients, except the chives, and cook for 5 more minutes.
3. Turn the duck breasts over again, raise the entire solution to a simmer and cook over medium heat for ten mins. Add the chives, distribute everything on the plates and serve.

BALSAMIC CHICKEN THIGHS

Preparation time: fifteen mins

Cooking time: 20 minutes

Servings: eight

Ingredients:

- 8 chicken thighs one teaspoon garlic powder
- one tsp. dried basil
- ½ teaspoon salt
- ½ teaspoon pepper
- 2 teaspoons dried minced onion
- 4 garlic cloves, minced
- 1 tablespoon olive oil
- ½ cup balsamic vinegar
- Fresh chopped parsley

Directions:

1. Join the initial 5 dry flavors in a touch bowl and unfold over chicken on the 2 aspects. Put in a secure spot.

2. Pour olive oil and garlic on the base of the moderate cooker.

3. Place the chicken on top.

4. Pour balsamic vinegar over the chicken.

5. Spread and cook dinner on LOW for 6 to 8 hours.

6. Sprinkle with crisp parsley on top. Serve over noodles.

DELICIOUS DESSERTS AND TREATS YOU CAN ENJOY GUILT-FREE

For individuals with kidney disease, adhering to a specific dietary regimen is vital for managing their condition and averting further harm. Two key nutrients that should be restricted in a kidney-friendly diet are sugar and potassium.

Excessive sugar consumption can escalate blood sugar levels, potentially leading to complications such as diabetes and cardiovascular disease. For individuals with kidney disease, elevated blood sugar can inflict additional harm to the kidneys. Hence, curtailing sugar intake and opting for kidney-friendly sweets is essential.

In the same vein, potassium is a mineral that is indispensable for various bodily processes, including nerve and muscle operations. However, for those suffering from kidney disease, surplus potassium in the bloodstream can be hazardous, causing issues such as arrhythmias and muscle weakness. As such, it's critical to limit potassium consumption and select kidney-friendly meals.

Regarding the selection of kidney-friendly desserts, it's crucial to seek out options that are low in both sugar and potassium.

Some recommendations for selecting kidney-friendly desserts encompass:

- Fruits such as apples, berries, and pineapples have lower potassium content and can be utilized in desserts like fruit salads or as yogurt toppings. Utilizing sugar alternatives Instead of regular sugar, contemplate using sugar alternatives like stevia or monk fruit sweetener. These options have fewer calories and assist in reducing sugar intake. Avoiding ingredients rich in potassium Certain ingredients that are high in potassium, including bananas, avocados, and dried fruit, should be omitted from desserts. Exploring low-sugar dessert options Consider low-sugar dessert options such as sugar-free jello, low-sugar cookies, and angel food cake. Mindful of portion sizes Even when consuming kidney-friendly desserts, being mindful of portion sizes is crucial. Overconsumption can result in elevated sugar and potassium intake, which can be detrimental for individuals with kidney disease.

FRUIT SALAD

Preparation time: 15 minutes

Cooking time: 0 minutes

Servings: 10

Ingredients:

- 1 cup canned pineapple chunks, drained
- 2 cups canned fruit cocktail, drained
- 1 cup sliced or whole strawberries hulled
- 1 cup marshmallows
- 1 cup peeled, cored, and chopped apple
- 1/2 cup non-dairy whipped topping

Directions:

1. Combine the entire fruits inside a container. Include the whipped topping and marshmallows. Mix well. Refrigerate for at least an hour. Serve chilled!

STRAWBERRY PIE

Preparation time: 15 mins

Cooking time: 20 mins

Servings: 8

Ingredients:

For the Crust:

- one and a half cups graham cracker crumbs
- 5 tbsp oil at room temperature
- 4 tbsp. stevia

For the Pie:

- 1 1/2 tsp gelatin powder
- 3 tbsp cornstarch
- 2 cup stevia
- 5 cups sliced strawberries, divided
- 1 cup water

Directions:

1. For the crust: heat your microwave to 375 F. Oil a pie pot. Combine the oil, crumbs, and stevia and press them into your pie pan.
2. Bake the crust for 10-15 minutes, 'til lightly browned. Take it out of the oven then let it cool completely.
3. For the pie, crush up a cup of strawberries. Combine the stevia, water, gelatin, and cornstarch using a small pot. Bring the mixture in the pot up to a boil, lower the heat, then simmer until it has thickened.
4. Add the crushed strawberries to the pot and allow it to simmer for another 5 mins till the sauce has thickened up

again. Set it off the heat and pour it into a bowl. Cool until it comes to room temperature.

5   Toss the remaining berries with the sauce to be well distributed, pour it into the pie crust, and spread it into an even layer. Refrigerate the pie until cold. It will take about 3 hours. Serve and enjoy!

SMALL CHOCOLATE CAKES

Preparation time: fifteen mins

Cooking time: 1 minute

Servings: 2

Ingredients:

- one box of angel food cake mix
- 1 box lemon cake mix
- Water
- Nonstick cooking spray or batter
- Dark chocolate small squared chops and chocolate powder

Directions:

1. Use a transparent kitchen cooking bag and put inside both lemon cake mixes, angel food mixes, and chocolate squared chops. Mix everything and put water to prepare a small cupcake.
2. Put the mix in a mold to prepare a cupcake containing the ingredients and put it in the microwave for a one-minute high temperature.
3. Slip the cupcake out of the mold, put it on a dish, let it cool, and put some more chocolate crumbs on it. Serve and relish!

SANDY CAKE

Preparation time: 1 hour

Cooking time: 50 minutes

Servings: 6

Ingredients:

- ½ cups starch
- 1 2/3 cups oil
- 3 cups stevia
- 3 whole eggs
- 1/2 sachet of yeast (2 tsps.)

Directions:

1. Combine the starch, whole eggs, oil, and stevia in a bowl.
2. Add the well-dissolved yeast and mix until the mixture becomes uniform.
3. Pour the mixture into the pan and put it in the oven.
4. Cooking time 40-50 min., At 180 ° C.

JEWELED COOKIES

Preparation time: 15 minutes

Cooking time: 10 minutes

Servings: 50 cookies

Ingredients:

- 1/2 cup softened unsalted margarine or oil
- 1 3/4 cups sifted all-purpose flour
- 2 cup stevia
- 1 medium egg
- 1 tsp vanilla
- 1/4 cup milk
- 1 tsp baking powder
- 15 large gumdrops

Directions:

1 Warm up your microwave to 400^0. Mix the egg, oil, and stevia thoroughly inside a container. Add in vanilla and milk, then stir.

2 Mix the flour & baking powder inside a different container. Add to the previous solution. Now include the gumdrops and mix, then chill for a minimum of one hour.

3 Spoon the dough using a tablespoon, then put it on an oiled cookie sheet. Bake for approximately 10 minutes or until it turns golden brown.

SWEET RASPBERRY CANDY

Preparation time: 5 minutes

Cooking time: 5 minutes

Servings: 12

Ingredients:

- 1/2 cup dried raspberries
- 3 tbsp swerve
- 1/2 cup coconut oil
- 2 oz cacao oil
- 1/2 tsp vanilla

Directions:

- Add cacao and coconut oil towards a pot and melt across low flame. Eliminate from flame.
- Grind the raspberries in a food processor.
- Add sweetener and ground raspberries into the melted oil and coconut oil mixture and stir well.
- Pour the mixture into the mini silicone candy molds and place them in the refrigerator until set.
- Serve & relish.

FROZEN LEMON DESSERT

Preparation time: fifteen mins

Cooking time: 10 mins

Servings: six

Ingredients:

- 4 eggs separated
- quarter cup lemon juice
- three cup stevia
- one tbsp lemon peel, grated
- 2 cups vanilla wafers, crushed
- 1 cup whipping cream, whipped

Directions:

1 Beat the egg yolks until it becomes very thick. Slowly add stevia and beat each time you add. Put the lemon peel and lemon juice, and mix well.

2 Put the batter in your double boiler, then cook over boiling water, continually stirring until the mixture gets thick. Set aside to cool.

3 Mix the egg whites until stiff peaks. Fold the egg whites into the thick mixture once cooled.

4 Add whipped cream and fold in. Spread one and a half crumbs of the vanilla wafer in the bottom of a baking dish or freezer tray.

5 Scoop the lemon mixture and spread over the crumbs. Sprinkle the remaining vanilla wafer crumbs on top. Fridge for several hours until the mixture is firm.

LEMON CAKE

Preparation time: 15 minutes

Cooking time: 1 hour & 20 minutes

Servings: 12

Ingredients:

- 2 cups oil
- 8 cups stevia
- 2 tsp grated lemon zest
- 1 tsp lemon extract
- 6 eggs
- 3 1/2 cups sifted all-purpose flour

Directions:

- Preheat your oven to 350 degrees. Cream oil on low speed with an electric mixer until light and fluffy.
- Slowly add in stevia and lemon zest; mix thoroughly. Add lemon extract and the eggs, one at a time, mixing after each addition.
- Add flour gradually and mix well. Pour batter into a greased & floured pan. Bake for one hour and 20 minutes. You will know it is done when a toothpick introduced in the cake center comes out clean.

SPRITZ COOKIES

Preparation time: 15 minutes

Cooking time: 8 minutes

Servings: 75 cookies

Ingredients:

- 5 cups all-purpose flour
- 2 cup + 4 tbsp stevia
- 2 cups oil
- 2 eggs
- 1 tsp almond extract
- 2 tsp vanilla extract

Directions:

1. Warm up your microwave to 400^0. Combine oil, flour, and stevia together. Put the vanilla almond extract and the eggs.
2. Mix the ingredients using a hand mixer at low speed. Put cookie batter into an ungreased baking sheet. Bake for about 8 minutes. Allow cooling prior to serving.

CHOCOLATE PIE SHELL

Preparation time: 15 minutes

Cooking time: 0 minutes

Servings: 6

Ingredients:

- 3 cups cocoa Krispies, crushed
- 4 tablespoon oil, ½ stickCooking spray

Directions:

1 Crush the cocoa Krispies, melt the oil, add both to a bowl, and stir. Oiled a 9-inch pie pan using cooking spray, then pressed the mixture into the pie pan.
2 Place in the refrigerator to chill for a minimum of 30 minutes before filling. You could add any filling of your choice

STRAWBERRY TIRAMISU

Preparation time: 15 minutes

Cooking time: 10 minutes

Servings: 4

Ingredients:

- 4 ladyfingers
- 3 tbsp almond syrup or amaretto
- 1 cup stevia
- 1/2 vanilla pod
- 4 oz. mascarpone
- 8 oz. cream quark
- 1 tbsp chopped pistachios
- 8 oz. strawberries

Directions:

1. Puree half of the strawberries with one tablespoon of stevia and the vanilla pulp. Cut the remaining strawberries into small pieces. Mix the mascarpone and cream quark with the remaining stevia.
2. Break the sponge fingers into pieces and divide them into four glasses. Pour almond syrup over it, then spread the strawberry puree and strawberries on top. Pour in the quark mixture and garnish with a piece of strawberry and pistachios.
3. Let soak in the fridge for an hr.

LEMON CRISPIES

Preparation time: 15 minutes

Cooking time: 10 minutes

Servings: 12

Ingredients:

- 1 cup unsalted margarine or oil
- 1 egg
- 2 cup stevia
- 1 1/2 tsp lemon extract
- 1 1/2 cups all-purpose flour, sifted

Directions:

1. Warm up your microwave to 375^0. Combine the oil and stevia. Add lemon extract and eggs to the mixture and beat until it becomes fluffy and light.
2. Add flour to the mixture and beat until smooth. Scoop the batter with a tablespoon and place it on an ungreased cookie sheet leaving at least a 2-inch space between the cookies.
3. Bake within 10 minutes or until the cookies turn brown around the edges. Allow the cookies to cool before you remove them from the cookie sheet

FRUIT CRUNCH

Preparation time: fifteen mins

Cooking time: 35 mins

Servings: 8

Ingredients:

- 4 tart apples, pare, core and slice
- two cup stevia
- 1/2 cup sifted all-purpose flour
- 1/3 cup margarine, softened
- 3/4 cup rolled oats
- 3/4 tsp nutmeg

Directions:

1. Preheat your oven to 375 degrees. Place the apples in a greased square 8-inch pan. Mix the other ingredients in a medium-sized bowl and spread the mixture over the apple. Bake within 35 minutes or until the Apple turns lightly brown and tender.

WHIPPED CREAM POUND CAKE

Preparation time: fifteen mins

Cooking time: 60 mins

Servings: 30 slices

Ingredients:

- two sticks of oil or margarine, softened
- 6 eggs
- 6 cups stevia
- 1/2-pint whipping cream
- 3 cups cake flour, sift once before you measure
- 1 tsp vanilla flavoring

Directions:

1 Preheat your oven to 350 degrees. Oil and flour in a tube/ baking pan. Ensure that all fixing is at room temperature. Mix stevia and margarine until fluffy.

2 Put the eggs one at a time, and beat before you add the next one. Slowly add the whipping cream and flour, mixing between each addition.

3 Beat the mixture for approximately 30 seconds, then stirs- in the vanilla flavoring. Put the batter into your greased and floured tube pan; bake for 60 minutes.

PINEAPPLE CAKE

Preparation time: 30 minutes

Cooking time: 45 minutes

Servings: 6

Ingredients:

For the Base:

- 4 oz. of flour
- 2 eggs
- 8 oz. of stevia
- 2 tsps. of vanilla yeast

For the Cream:

- 1 whole egg, 1 yolk
- 1 cup stevia
- 3 tablespoons flour
- 4 cups semi-skimmed milk
- 10 oz. pineapple
- 8 oz. cream for desserts
- Grated lemon zest

Directions:

1 To prepare the base of the cake, you have to work the flour, stevia, and yeast until a homogeneous mixture. Bake at 160 degrees for about 15 minutes. After baking, let the cake cool.
2 Meanwhile, prepare the cream. In a saucepan, place on low heat; beat a whole egg and the yolk with the stevia and flour.
3 Add the milk lukewarm previously brought to a boil, with 1/2 grated lemon zest.

4 Cook everything on a slow fire, stirring for about 4-5 minutes.

5 When the base has cooled, cut the upper part (2/3 sup.), pour on the bottom of the pineapple juice (from the can), then put the prepared cream and a layer of cream.

6 Finally, cover them with the mixture from crumbling the unused part of the cake (the smaller one) combined with the pineapple cut into small pieces.

7 Before serving, the cake must be inside the refrigerator for two hrs.

www.ingramcontent.com/pod-product-compliance
Lightning Source LLC
LaVergne TN
LVHW050645200726
843506LV00010B/1368